ANIMAL
OLYMPICS

Lizzie Lizard's
Long Jump

by Enid Richemont and Inna Chernyak

W

F

For David Richemont, with love E.R.

Franklin Watts
First published in Great Britain in 2016
by the Watts Publishing Group

ISBN 978 1 4451 4779 6 (hbk)
ISBN 978 1 4451 4781 9 (pbk)
ISBN 978 1 4451 4780 2 (library ebook)

Series Editor: Melanie Palmer
Series Advisor: Catherine Glavina
Series Designer: Peter Scoulding

Printed in China

Franklin Watts
an imprint of Hachette Children's Group
Part of the Watts Publishing Group
Carmelite House
50 Victoria Embankment
London EC4Y 0DZ

An Hachette UK company
www.hachette.co.uk

www.franklinwatts.co.uk

Lizzie Lizard was training
for the long jump.
She knew she could win
if she did her best.

Harry Hawk was out hunting. He liked lizards. "Let's meet," he said, hungrily.

"Not now," said Lizzie,
"I'm jumping."

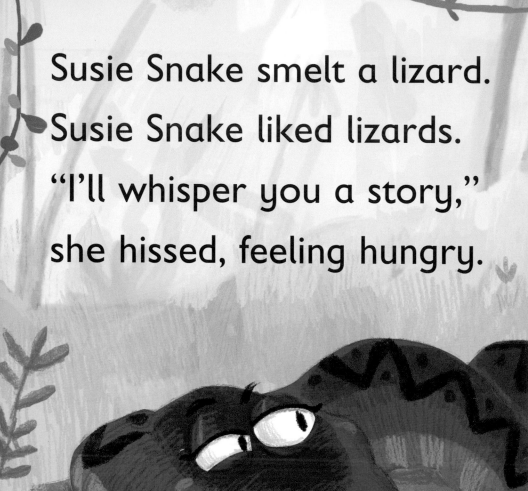

Susie Snake smelt a lizard.
Susie Snake liked lizards.
"I'll whisper you a story,"
she hissed, feeling hungry.

"Not now," said Lizzie
Lizard. "I'm jumping."

Rocky Raccoon saw Lizzie and felt hungry. "I've got a pretty beetle," he said. "Want to see?"

Lizzie Lizard sighed.
"Not now," she said,
"I'm jumping."

Lizzie landed on a faraway rock. Harry Hawk swooped ...

... but Lizzie jumped.

Lizzie landed on some
ferns. Susie Snake
slid over.

"Now you have to listen to my story," Susie hissed.

"Because ..." she
grabbed Lizzie
"... I've got your tail!"

"Keep it! I'll grow another one," said Lizzie, jumping away.

Rocky Raccoon started jumping too.

"Watch out, Lizzie!" he cried. "I can jump further than you."

Lizzie aimed for a hollow, high up in a tree. "This would be my longest jump ever!" she thought. "Can I do it?"

At the same time,
Lennie Leopard spotted
Rocky. Lennie Leopard
licked his lips.

"Watch out, Rocky!" he roared. "I can jump further than you."

Rocky tried to grab Lizzie,
but Lizzie jumped.
"Whee!" she cried.

"That was the best long jump ever!" cried Lizzie's brothers and sisters.

"Not as good as Rocky's,"
said Lizzie. "Look!"

START

5 | 6

Puzzle 1

a

b

c

d

e

f

Put these pictures in the correct order.
Now tell the story in your own words.
How short can you make the story?

busy   scared
fearless

hungry   nasty
friendly

Choose the words which best describe the characters. Can you think of any more? Pretend to be one of the characters!

Answers

Puzzle 1

The correct order is:

1f, 2b, 3e, 4a, 5d, 6c

Puzzle 2

The correct words are busy, fearless.

The incorrect word is scared.

The correct words are hungry, nasty.

The incorrect word is friendly.

Look out for more stories:

Mary and the Fairy
ISBN 978 0 7496 9142 4

The Bossy Cockerel
ISBN 978 0 7496 9141 7

Tim's Tent
ISBN 978 0 7496 7801 2

Sticky Vickie
ISBN 978 0 7496 7986 6

Handyman Doug
ISBN 978 0 7496 7987 3

Billy and the Wizard
ISBN 978 0 7496 7985 9

Sam's Spots
ISBN 978 0 7496 7984 2

Bill's Scary Backpack
ISBN 978 0 7496 9468 5

Bill's Silly Hat
ISBN 978 1 4451 1617 4

Little Joe's Boat Race
ISBN 978 0 7496 9467 8

Little Joe's Horse Race
ISBN 978 1 4451 1619 8

Felix and the Kitten
ISBN 978 0 7496 7988 0

Felix, Puss in Boots
ISBN 978 1 4451 1621 1

Cheeky Monkey's Big Race
ISBN 978 1 4451 1618 1

The Naughty Puppy
ISBN 978 0 7496 9145 5

Prickly Ballroom
ISBN 978 0 7496 9475 3

The Animals' Football Cup
ISBN 978 0 7496 9477 7

The Animals' Football Camp
ISBN 978 1 4451 1616 7

That Noise!
ISBN 978 0 7496 9479 1

The Wrong House
ISBN 978 0 7496 9480 7

The Frog Prince and the Kitten
ISBN 978 1 4451 1620 4

For details of all our titles go to: www.franklinwatts.co.uk